MISTER BOFFO
"IT ONLY TAKES A LITTLE BIT OF GREED TO GET A WHOLE LOT OF STUFF"
AND HIS WONDER-DOG "WEEDERMAN"
BY JOE MARTIN
I SAW YOUR OLD BOYFRIEND AT THE DRIVE-UP WINDOW OF THE BANK TODAY...
WHAT A LOSER!
HE DROVE AWAY WITH THEIR CARRIER TUBE!...
AND MADE A TOTAL FOOL OF HIMSELF WHEN HE HAD TO DRIVE BACK AND GIVE IT TO THE TELLER!
WHAT WERE YOU DOING AT THE BANK?!
I WAS WIPING WINDSHIELDS FOR BEER MONEY.
JOE MARTIN

AF731761

THE VERY WORST THING THAT CAN HAPPEN TO SOMEONE TWELVE OR UNDER
MUSEUM of HOMEWORK AND VEGETABLES
JOE MARTIN

OPTOMETRISTS UNCLEAR ON THE CONCEPT
THERE, PINHEAD!. DOES IT STILL LOOK LIKE A "B"!!?
ACBFS
BLTRN
JOE MARTIN

"TIME-SAVER TIP OF THE WEEK" AWARD
I'LL DEAL FOR THE CAT... IT'LL MOVE FASTER.
JOE MARTIN

PEOPLE UNCLEAR ON THE CONCEPT
THAT'S HER!..THAT'S HER!...I'D RECOGNIZE THAT PURSE ANYWHERE!!
JOE MARTIN

LEAST LIKELY TO JUDGE INTERNATIONAL WINE COMPETITIONS
POP
THONK
AH, YES..VERY GOOD... THAT WILL DO NICELY.
JOE MARTIN

JOE MARTIN

MISTER BOFFO
FZZZT
FZZZT
BZZT
BZZZT
RRRR
GRRRRRRRRRR
SPWOP
IGOR!!..
YOU IDIOT!..
JOE MARTIN
GRRREAAAAA
THIS IS THE BRAIN OF A MAN I OWE FIVE THOUSAND DOLLARS TO!!

"BUY HIGH, SELL LOW"... I RODE THAT IDEA RIGHT INTO THE TOILET!
JOE MARTIN

THE FURTHER ADVENTURES OF SHERLOCK HOLMES' IDIOT SON EARL
I FOUND THE SECRET COMPARTMENT BEHIND THE MIRROR WHERE YOU KEEP YOUR TOILETRIES!

EARL "TWO-CAN-PLAY AT-THAT-GAME" BOFFO
FOOSH
SSSSSSS
JOE MARTIN

MISTER BOFFO
"HARD WORK IS NATURE'S WAY OF SAYING 'YOU DO IT'"
I DON'T DRINK..
I DON'T SMOKE..
I HAVEN'T TASTED RED MEAT FOR NINE YEARS
AND EVERY HALF-HOUR I WHACK MYSELF IN THE HEAD WITH A HAMMER
JOE MARTIN

ANOTHER REASON WHY IT'S NOT ALWAYS A GOOD IDEA TO DRIVE WITH SOMEONE WHO HAS SUICIDAL TENDENCIES
CLEAR ON MY SIDE...
JOE MARTIN

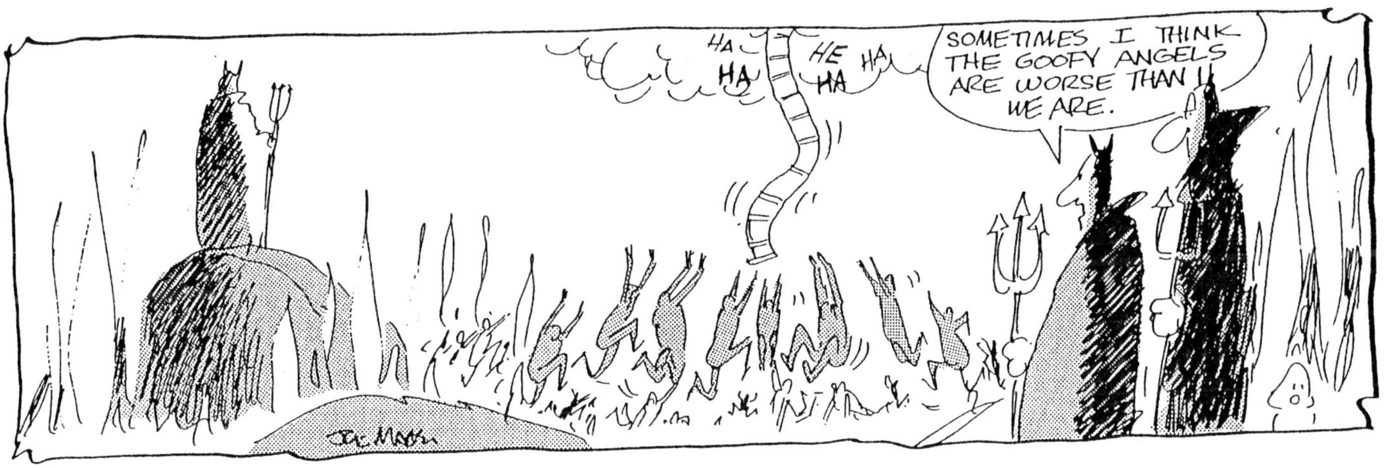
HA HA
HE HA
HA
SOMETIMES I THINK THE GOOFY ANGELS ARE WORSE THAN WE ARE.

THE OLD ARMY BUDDY, THE PLASTIC SURGEON AND THE LAWSUIT
JOE MARTIN

I. FETCH
II. SIT
III. SPEAK
IV. GO
V. STAY
VI PAW
VII ROLL OVER
VIII POINT
IX PLAY DEAD
X HEEL
JOE MARTIN

THE YOUNG RAND MCNALLY
TURN HERE.
JOE MARTIN

SOON-TO-BE-UNEMPLOYED UPDATE
DO YOU HAVE ANY NAMED "FREDDIE"?
NO, I'M SORRY... ALL THE "FREDDIES" HAVE BEEN SOLD
JOE MARTIN

UP
JOE MARTIN
" HANDCUFFED TO THE BARS OF A CARDBOARD PRISON,
HE WAITS OUT HIS TIME LIKE THE FOOL HE IS "

PUTTING THINGS IN THE BEST POSSIBLE WAY
KIESTERMITIS!?
JOE MARTIN

I WAS WONDERING IF THEY MIGHT DO SOMETHING SPECIAL FOR MY BIRTHDAY THIS YEAR.
JOE MARTIN
ANOTHER WAY TO TELL WHEN YOU'RE DEALING WITH SOMEONE WHO HASN'T BEEN IN THE LIZARD POT YET

CLIFF DIVER WITH A RUBBER HEAD
JOE MARTIN

WORST PIECE OF MILITARY STRATEGY AWARD: MIME FRONT LINE GIVING THE ENEMY THE IMPRESSION OF AN INVISIBLE IMPENETRABLE WALL
READY... AIM...
JOE MARTIN

MAN WHO LOST HIS JOB, HIS WIFE AND HIS FAVORITE TIE-PIN ON THE SAME DAY
JOE MARTIN

PEOPLE UNCLEAR ON THE CONCEPT
VERY GOOD, CLASS... NOW, WHERE WOULD YOU STAND IF THE MISSILE WITH THE NUCLEAR WARHEAD WERE TO LAND... OVER HERE !?
JOE MARTIN

THE KIND OF THING YOU HATE TO SEE AFTER TAKING THE PAINS TO LEAD A GOOD AND HONEST LIFE
JOE MARTIN

A TIME TO WORRY
JOE MARTIN

THE TAILOR HERE MUST BE ONE OF US
JOE MARTIN

A BIG PART OF THE REASON THE ENTIRE RACE OF MICRO-MIDGETS WAS WIPED OFF THE FACE OF THE EARTH BY THE BONE GIANTS
WELL, WELL... IF IT ISN'T PORKHEAD !!
JOE MARTIN

AND THIS ONE I GOT FOR BEING THE FIRST ONE AT THE GARAGE SALE!
JOE MARTIN

THE KIND OF THING YOU HATE TO FIND FLOATING IN YOUR TOILET

AT FIRST WE CALLED HIM "CHIRPY".. THEN IT WAS "WHEEZY"... THEN "SLEEPY".. THEN "SMELLY"... AND NOW FOR THE LONGEST TIME IT'S BEEN "BONES"
JOE MARTIN

WE FORGOT TO FACTOR IN HOW MUCH THE 1'S LOOK LIKE L'S.
JOE MARTIN

THREE MEN FALLING DOWN BOTTOMLESS PIT
SAME 3 GUYS 6 MONTHS LATER
JOE MARTIN

A TIME TO WORRY
WILL WORK FOR AMMO
JOE MARTIN

THE REASON WHY THEY HAVE MOTHERS
OK... DO ALL YOUR HOMEWORK, TAKE YOUR BATH, BRUSH YOUR TEETH REAL GOOD...
AND I'LL LET YOU STAY UP WITH ME AND WATCH T.V. AND EAT POPCORN TILL THE SUN COMES UP...
AND TOMORROW WE'LL SLEEP IN!
JOE MARTIN

MAKING THE BEST OF A BAD SITUATION
BREAD
ON OFF
LIGHT • DARK
JOE MARTIN

PRACTICAL JOKERS UNCLEAR ON THE CONCEPT
I THOUGHT YOU SAID YOU TURNED THE COFFEE POT OFF ?!
GOTCHA!
JOE MARTIN

A TIME TO WORRY
JOE MARTIN
ME AND SOME OF THE GUYS ARE GOING UP NORTH FOR A FEW WEEKS OF FISHING, HUNTING AND SERIOUS CARD PLAYING...
POP
FIZZZ

LIFE'S EMBARRASSING MOMENTS
WELL, IF IT WAS A WHOOPEE-CUSHION... LET'S SEE IT
JOE MARTIN

SEVENTEEN ARRESTS, SEVENTEEN CONVICTIONS..
MAYBE IT IS ME
JOE MARTIN

NEVER HAVE I HEARD THE WORD "YOWZA" USED WITH MORE FEELING!
JOE MARTIN

THE FIRST DAY
WHAT THE HECK WAS THAT!

DOES IT STRIKE YOU AS STRANGE THAT I DO ALL THE TALKING?
JOE MARTIN

DONUTS 25¢
I'D LIKE TWENTY THOUSAND CHOCOLATE DONUTS PLEASE
DONUTS 25¢
HIT THE BRICKS, KID, WE'RE NOT FALLING FOR THAT ONE AGAIN
JOE MARTIN

YOU'D THINK A GUY THAT GOOD WITH A SLING SHOT WOULD BE QUICKER ON HIS FEET
JOE MARTIN

" WHAT EVER HAPPENED TO EARTHQUAKES AND TORNADOES !? "

CROMC
COSGROVE
MASTER OF THE UNEXPECTED
JOE MARTIN

MOST UNEXPECTED BAD NEWS AWARD
EVERYTHING WENT FINE.. THE BABY SLEPT THE WHOLE TIME .. BUT THERE WAS SOME STATIC ON THE TELEVISION, I THOUGHT IT MIGHT BE THE DOG.. SO I HAD HIM PUT TO SLEEP
JOE MARTIN

FIRST TIME ?
JOE MARTIN

ZOT
NICE TRY, WEASEL!
XI THOU SHALT GIVE MOSES HALF OF EVERYTHING
JOE MARTIN

I DON'T SUPPOSE YOU'D LIKE TO SEE THE TEST RESULTS
M.D
JOE MARTIN

THE VERY WORST THING AN INMATE CAN POSSIBLY DO DURING A JAIL BREAK
PSSST—
BYE.
WARDEN
JOE MARTIN

MISTER BOFFO
"MOE"
AND HIS WONDER-DOG "WEEDERMAN"
-THE CHOSEN ONE -
BY JOE MARTIN
WEEDERMAN... IF ONLY YOU COULD TALK... THE WORLD WOULD BE OUR OYSTER...
WE COULD HAVE IT ALL IF YOU COULD JUST SAY ONE LITTLE WORD...
JUST ONE WORD, THAT'S ALL... ANY WORD!
UNDERPANTS.
WELL... MAYBE NOT ANY WORD.
JOE MARTIN

THE COLONEL IN HELL
OOPS... SORRY!
YEAH... RIGHT

HEART BUTTS IN LOVE
JOE MARTIN

SLEPT IN FRONT OF DOOR TODAY
my Diary
FEB. 20
slept in front of door today
my Diary
FEB. 21
slept in front of door today
JOE MARTIN

SHRINK-
WRAPPED
JOE MARTIN

I WANT TO KEEP ACCURATE NOTES.. IS ONE "BLAH-BLAH" ENOUGH OR DO I HAVE TO WRITE DOWN ALL TWENTY-FOUR THOUSAND ?
FULLBEAN INC.
JOE MARTIN

ANOTHER WAY TO TELL WHEN YOUR RELATIONSHIP'S IN TROUBLE
DO YOU MIND IF I HUM WHEN YOU TALK ?... IT HELPS ME CONCENTRATE

PEOPLE UNCLEAR ON THE CONCEPT
HERE COMES MY RIDE
JOE MARTIN

THE GOOD NEWS IS WE GOT THE CHARGES REDUCED TO METER FEEDING
JOE MARTIN
THE BAD NEWS IS YOU'LL BE THE FIRST MAN IN THIS STATE TO BE EXECUTED FOR A PARKING VIOLATION

MISTER BOFFO
"SWIMSUIT EDITION"
-PLAYBOY'S LOWEST SELLING ISSUE-
AND HIS WONDER-DOG "WEEDERMAN"
BY JOE MARTIN
LEON'S
CARRY OUT BEER
I USED TO THINK THERE WAS ONLY ONE RIGHT WAY TO DRINK BEER!
FROSTED MUG... JUST THE RIGHT TEMPERATURE WITH NO MORE THAN A ONE-INCH HEAD ON IT!
BUT THEN MY NEPHEW, PLAYING A JOKE, GAVE ME A WARM CAN THAT HE'D BEEN SHAKING FOR FIFTEEN MINUTES...
AND THAT TASTED PRETTY GOOD TOO!
JOE MARTIN

THE BEST OF
Willy 'n Ethel

JOE MARTIN

"IT'S OK .. I'M WATCHING HIM"

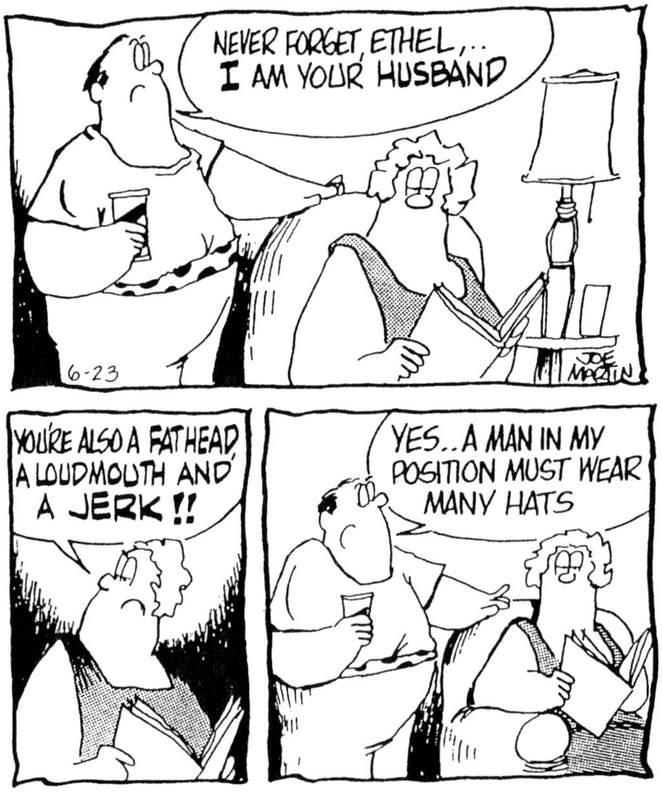

"THERE YOU ARE!! I THOUGHT YOU WERE HOME! YA KNOW, WE ALMOST LEFT WHEN YOU DIDN'T ANSWER THE DOOR!"

"HALF OF ME SAID 'DUCK,' BUT THE OTHER HALF SAID 'WHAT IF IT'S BLUEBERRY?'"

"HE USED TO THINK THE WHOLE WORLD WAS AGAINST HIM, BUT NOW HE'S NARROWED IT DOWN TO ONE GUY WITH A HOSE"

"THIS BETTER NOT BE ANOTHER FIRE HYDRANT"

"MAYBE YOU SHOULD TRY THE ONE WITH THE CLOWN ON IT"

"WELL, WE TOOK A CHANCE.. WE GAMBLED... AND WE LOST!"

" ISN'T THIS THE SAME WAY 'JAWS I' ENDED ?"

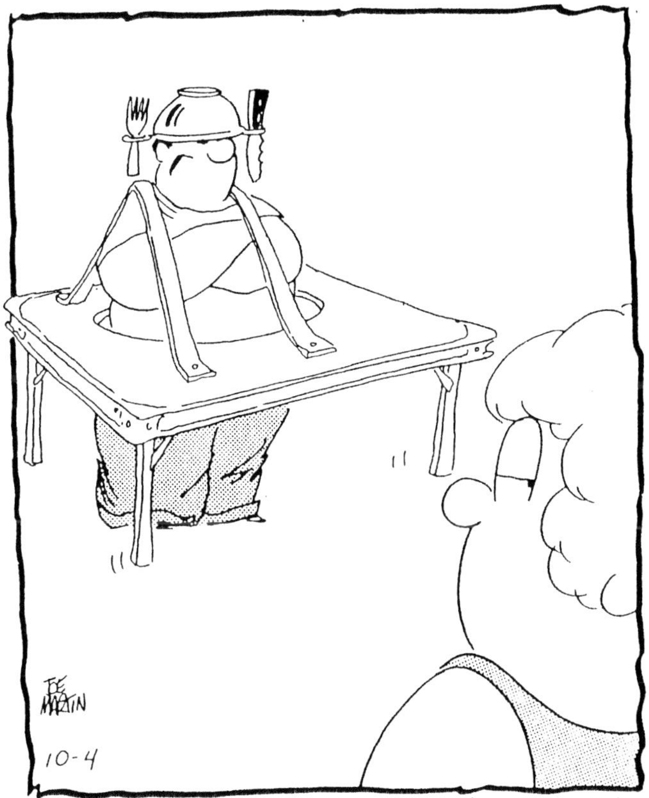

" WELL, ETHEL, DO YOU STILL THINK I'M CRAZY ? "

STOP AT
Vito's
Food + Lodging
"JUST 2 MI. NORTH OF THE SHORT FAT GUY SITTING ON THE STEPS DRINKING BEER"
6-19
JOE MARTIN

DAD
MOM
I THINK YOUR FOLKS ARE HINTING THAT YOU SHOULD VISIT THEM MORE OFTEN
DAD
MOM
MY FOLKS!? I THOUGHT THEY WERE YOUR FOLKS!
6-24
JOE MARTIN

IF I SWALLOW A WATERMELON SEED WILL IT GROW IN MY STOMACH?
9-27
LISTEN, KID, I'M A DOCTOR, NOT A FARMER
JOE MARTIN

"BEATS ME HOW A GUY CAN MAKE A LIVING SELLING ONE WORM AT A TIME"

"THE CHEF'S GOING THROUGH SOME SERIOUS PERSONAL PROBLEMS RIGHT NOW AND WE'RE TRYING TO BE AS SUPPORTIVE AS POSSIBLE"

"HIS LIFE SAVINGS IS FIFTY CENTS... THAT'S JUST WALKING-AROUND MONEY FOR ME AND YOU"

"HOLD ON!"

" HE THROWS THE STICKS IN THE AIR, I WAVE THE BAGS... IT'S ALL SO MEANINGLESS "

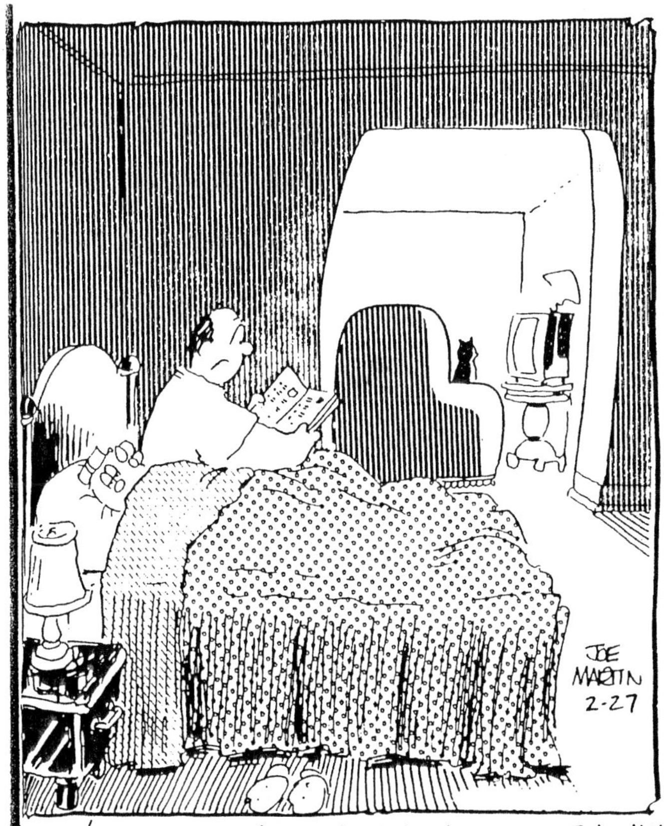

THERE'S NOTHING ON.. NOTHING AT ALL... JUST JUNK! THAT CAT'S NUTS!! "

"IS THAT AS FAR AS YOU CAN THROW ?!"

"YOUR NEPHEW TOOK YOUR CAMERA APART, CLEANED THE LENSES, ADJUSTED THE SHUTTERS, REALIGNED THE GEARS, AND NOW IT'S A PAPERWEIGHT"

"WELL, WELL, WELL... THE OL' 'BALLOON-COVERED-WITH-GRAVY' TRICK"

"FROM NOW ON, FINNEGAN, LET THE BALD-HEADED PEOPLE SIT WHEREVER THEY WANT!"

"SURE, SCRAPE EVERY SHRED OF MEAT OFF THE BONE, THEN COME BACK TOMORROW AND COMPLAIN ABOUT THE SOUP BEIN' WEAK"

"C'MON, ETHEL, IT'S NINETY DEGREES!.. LET SOMEONE ELSE LOOK FOR THE MUSTARD!!"

"I BELIEVE YOU'VE MADE A MISTAKE IN OUR ACCOUNT... ACTUALLY MY HUSBAND WAS THE FIRST TO NOTICE"

"YOUR SIDE OF THE FAMILY WOULD HAVE A LOT MORE FUN IF THEY'D LOOSEN UP A LITTLE AND TRY TO GET CONTROL OF THE HOSE"

" NOW TRY IT "

"YA KNOW, YOU'RE RIGHT... THIS ISN'T AS EASY AS IT LOOKS"

"HERE COMES ANOTHER ONE THAT CAN'T READ"

"CAPITALIZE 'CREDIT MANAGER,' PUT A COMMA BETWEEN 'ADDITIONAL LIABILITIES' AND 'FINANCIAL PRESSURE,' A PERIOD AFTER 'REALIGN INSTALL-MENT SCHEDULE' AND HYPHENATE 'PIG-FACE'."

"OK, GENIUS, IT'S MY MOTHER, THINK FAST! WHY AM I LIVING IN A BASEMENT WITH A FAT DWARF?"

"SO, IT'S ANOTHER TAILGATER, IS IT?!! RIDING RIGHT ON MY BUMPER!!
WELL, WILLY, YOU KNOW HOW I HANDLE THESE CLOWNS!!

"OK, LET'S SPEED THINGS UP AND SET A TWENTY-MINUTE LIMIT ON THE SHAKING OF THE DICE"

"IT WAS MUCH BETTER THE LAST TIME WE WERE HERE... OF COURSE THEN WE WERE CLOSER TO THE FRONT WHERE IT'S NOT SO PICKED OVER"

GOOD NEWS AND BAD NEWS, UNCLE WILLY... FIRST THE GOOD NEWS...
YOU CAN STOP LOOKING FOR THAT GAS STATION
4-17
JOE MARTIN

"'THE EARTH SHOOK, THE SKY RUMBLED, AND A VOICE SAID, "NOAH, IF YOU MISUNDERSTAND ME ONE MORE TIME I'M GOING TO MAKE IT RAIN FOR 40 DAYS AND 40 NIGHTS... NOW GO OUT AND GATHER TWO OF EVERY ANIMAL IN THE WORLD AND BUILD FOR THEM A GIANT PARK."'"

YOU'RE NEVER GONNA GET A JOB... YOU'RE JUST GONNA LIE THERE AND DO NOTHING... SLEEP! SLEEP! SLEEP! THAT'S ALL YOU'RE EVER GONNA DO!!
3·11
JOE MARTIN
DON'T STOP

"DON'T HIT THAT SNACK TRAY TOO HEAVY... I WAS JUST KIDDING WHEN I SAID WE WERE INVITED"

"THAT'S NOT AN 'AUTOMATIC' CHANNEL CHANGER INTERCEPTOR, IS IT ?"

"LIFT THAT GATE, BOY, IT'S TOLL GATE TOMMY... HE RIDES FREE!"

Joe Martin

"OK, WE'LL PUT IT TO A VOTE...WHAT WOULD YOU RATHER DO ?..FLOAT AIMLESSLY FOR DAYS OR GO REAL FAST FOR A FEW SECONDS ? "

AL'S
HOME OF THE WORLD'S
GREATEST STEW
CHILI
SOUP
TEA
CATSUP
WATER
CARD TRICKS
SPFTTT

"OH, NO!"

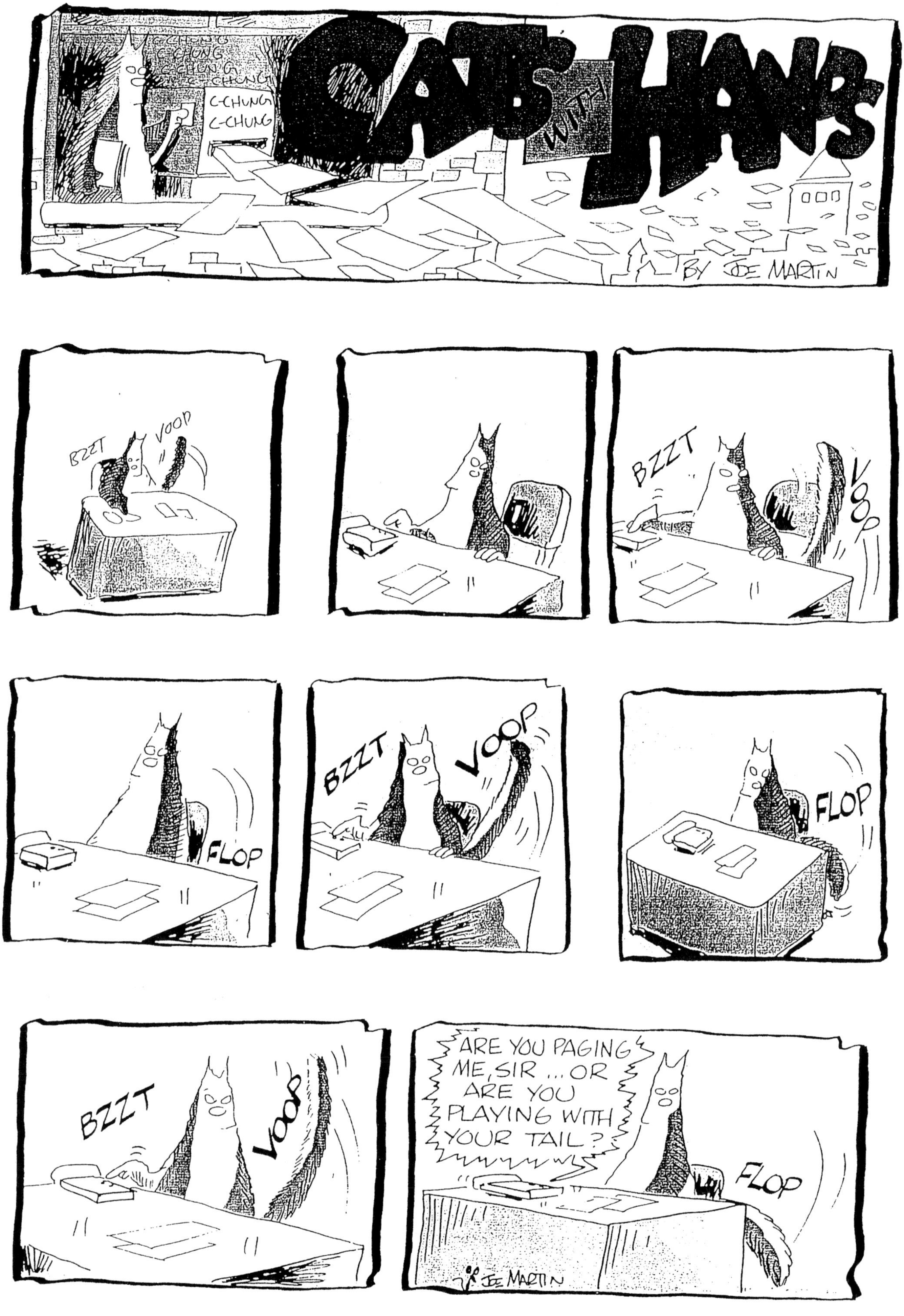

C-CHUNG
C-CHUNG
C-CHUNG
C-CHUNG
C-CHUNG
C-CHUNG
CATS WITH HANDS
BY JOE MARTIN
BZZT
VOOP
BZZT
VOOP
FLOP
BZZT
VOOP
FLOP
BZZT
VOOP
ARE YOU PAGING ME, SIR ... OR ARE YOU PLAYING WITH YOUR TAIL?
FLOP
JOE MARTIN

WRONG PERSON TO ASK AWARD
WHEN IS IT OKAY TO USE A BLOWTORCH TO TRIM YOUR WHISKERS?
WHEN ISN'T IT?!
JOE MARTIN 11-27-00

THE ENEMY WITHIN
JOE MARTIN

MISS HASTINGS ... HAVE THEM OPEN THE BACK DOOR ... ID LIKE TO GO OUT FOR A WHILE
JOE MARTIN

IF SIR EDMUND HILARY AND HIS SHERPA GUIDE, TENZIG NORGAY, WERE CATS
EDDY
TENZY
JOE MARTIN
© 1999 Joe Martin

THE MOUSE WHISPERER
JOE MARTIN

90% OF THE PROJECT IS HAVING THE RIGHT TOOLS
© 1999 Joe Martin.
JOE MARTIN

© 1999 Joe Martin.
I'VE FAILED AT EVERYTHING I EVER KIND OF SHOWED A PASSING INTEREST IN TRYING FOR A LITTLE WHILE
JOE MARTIN

NUMBER ONE ON LIST OF WAYS TO TELL THERE'S BEEN AN OPERATION
STUD MUFFIN
JOE MARTIN
© 1999 Joe Martin.

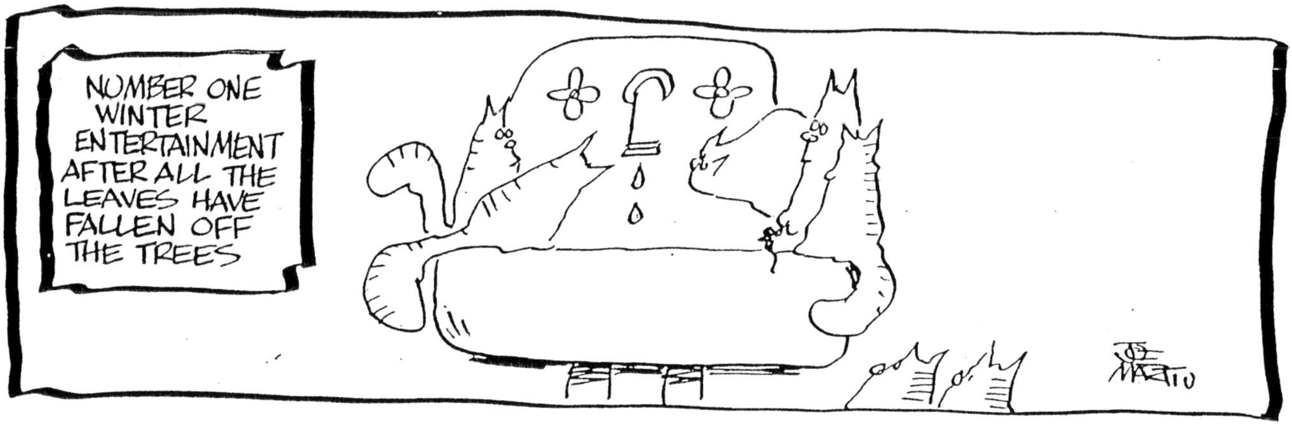
NUMBER ONE WINTER ENTERTAINMENT AFTER ALL THE LEAVES HAVE FALLEN OFF THE TREES
JOE MARTIN

ARE YOU STILL UPSET OVER THE ARGUMENT WE HAD AT DINNER... OR DO YOU JUST WANT TO GO OUT?
© 2000 Joe Martin
JOE MARTIN 5-22-00

ARE YOU RAISING YOUR HAND TO ASK A QUESTION, OR ARE YOU MAKING SHADOWS ON THE WALL
ACTUALLY I DO HAVE A QUESTION... BUT IT IS ABOUT MAKING HAND SHADOWS
JOE MARTIN 11-3-00
© 2000 Joe Martin.

SLOWLY, VERY SLOWLY STEP BACK TOWARD THE KITCHEN AND GET ME THE TENDERIZER
JOE MARTIN 7-17-00

SHOE LACES, YARN, JINGLE BALL STRING, RUBBER MOUSE...
WHAT AM I FORGETTING?
JOE MARTIN

© 1999 Joe Martin.
THE MAIN PROBLEM WITH THESE FORMAL DINNER DANCES IS KICKING OVER THE FOOD BOWLS
CLONK
CLONK
CLONK
CLONK
CLONK
JOE MARTIN

YOU'RE STEREOTYPING YOURSELF... YOU REALIZE THAT, DON'T YOU?!
JOE MARTIN

© 1999 Joe Martin.
BEFORE LIFE RAFTS HAD SCRATCHING POSTS
S.S. KITTY
JOE MARTIN

SO THEN IT'S UNANIMOUS... WE EIGHTY-SIX THE CHAIRS
JOE MARTIN

HE SITS LIKE THAT ALL DAY EVERY DAY... STARING INTO SPACE... NEVER EVEN BLINKS
HE'S GOOD, REAL GOOD... I'VE NEVER SEEN BETTER

OK... IN THIS SITUATION LOOKING LIKE YOU MEANT TO DO IT DEFINITELY WORKS AGAINST YOU!
JOE MARTIN

© 2000 Joe Martin.
HOLD IT A SECOND... I LIKE MINE WITH CHEESE
JOE MARTIN 10-9-00

I'M YOUR GREAT AUNT ON YOUR MOTHER'S SIDE, FIRST COUSIN'S NEPHEW'S WIFE'S COUSIN'S SISTERS NIECE'S KID
WHO ISN'T?
JOE MARTIN 9-1-00
© 2000 Joe Martin.

DUAL HONOR OF THE WEEK
MOST OFTEN REPEATED PHRASE
& MOST FITTING NICKNAME
STAND STILL, "JITTERS"
JOE MARTIN
© 2000 Joe Martin.
3-8-00

IT'S DOPEY CAT.!.
C'MON, DOPEY CAT... TRY AND CATCH ME...
C'MON, DOPEY CAT,... I'M RIGHT HERE!.. COME AND GET ME, DOPEY CAT!
MAN... CAN THIS GUY DANCE!
© 2000 Joe Martin.
JOE MARTIN
4-3-00

© 2000 Joe Martin.
GAS
FLUFFY'S
CAR REPAIR
WHENEVER I GO OVER FIFTY, IT MAKES THIS LITTLE PINGING NOISE... LIKE SOMEONE'S FILLING MY BOWL
JOE MARTIN
3-27-00

I DON'T KNOW IF I'D BE SMILING IF I WAS IN THAT PREDICAMENT
JOE MARTIN

"LUCA BRAZZI SLEEPS WITH THE FISHES!"
NOW THAT'S THE WAY I WANT TO GO!
© 1999 Joe Martin
JOE MARTIN

NEXT TIME WE HAVE TO REMEMBER TO ORDER IT MEDIUM RARE
VOOP
© 2000 Joe Martin. Dist. by
JOE MARTIN
3-7-00

3-10-00
UNDERSTATEMENT OF THE YEAR
HE'S A ONE-IN-A-MILLION!
© 2000 Joe Martin.
JOE MARTIN

ANOTHER WAY TO TELL WHEN YOU'RE DEALING WITH ONE OF THE REGULARS
JOE MARTIN 10-5-00
© 2000 Joe Martin.

UNDERSTATEMENT OF THE WEEK AWARD
OK... WATCH YOUR PIECES... THIS GAME MOVES FAST!
JOE MARTIN 5-20-00
© 2000 Joe Martin.

I ALWAYS HAVE TO CIRCLE THE BLOCK A FEW TIMES BEFORE I CAN GET COMFORTABLE ENOUGH TO SETTLE INTO A PARKING SPOT
WHO DOESN'T?
JOE MARTIN 3-24-00
© 2000 Joe Martin.

I'LL TELL YOU THIS OUT FRONT... IF YOU CAME HERE EXPECTING TO SIT AROUND AND DO NOTHING... ALL THE GOOD SPOTS HAVE ALREADY BEEN TAKEN!
EMPLOYMENT
JOE MARTIN 7-6-00
© 2000 Joe Martin.

THE KIND OF THING THAT CAN PUT A DAY ON THE PLUS SIDE OF THE LEDGER
8-25-00
BOF
BOF
BOF
JOE MARTIN © 2000 Joe Martin.

DING DING DING DING DING DING DING DING
IT'S LIKE I'M CONSTANTLY BEING PAGED
JOE MARTIN

FINDING OUT THE HARD WAY ABOUT THE TRANS-DIMENSIONAL SPACE WARP BEHIND THE KITCHEN RADIATOR

EMPLOYMENT OFFICE
"FLUFFY"?!
IT'S SHORT FOR FLUFFENSTEIN

JUST WHEN I THINK I'M OUT, THEY PULL ME BACK AGAIN
MUFFIN CORLEON
JOE MARTIN

Felix Felix
RESUME SERVICE
"HOUSE BROKEN" IS A BIG DEAL WITH DOGS... BUT FOR US IT'S EXPECTED... I WOULDN'T EVEN INCLUDE IT
JOE MARTIN

© 2000 Joe Martin
JOE MARTIN
1-12-2000
THE MARK OF ZIPPY

SURVIVALIST MOUSE OF THE YEAR
BEFORE YOU DO THAT, CAN I ASK YOU ONE FAVOR?.. TAKE A LOOK AT THIS ODD SHAPED MOLE AND TELL ME IF YOU THINK IT'S ANYTHING
JOE MARTIN 1-14-2000
© 2000 Joe Martin.

AND THIS IS WHERE WE KEEP THE FISH
JOE MARTIN 1-26-2000
© 2000 Joe Martin.

BAD NEWS FOR THE SUPPORTERS OF THE "DAILY MEWS"
WE'VE BEEN OUT-VOTED... THEY SAID IT WAS "TOO CUTESY."..
THEY'RE GOING WITH EITHER "CHRONICLE," "TIMES," OR "TRIBUNE"
© 1999 Joe Martin.
JOE MARTIN

UNION BENEFITS SEMINAR
MAIN HALL
TODAY'S TOPIC
TREATS
TREATS
TREATS
JOE MARTIN
© 1999 Joe Martin.

THE WORLD AND THE WAY IT WOULD BE IF A CAT WERE ELECTED PRESIDENT

ADAM AND EVE AND THE FIRST SUGGESTION BOX
FRIDAY FISH FRY
A+E
JOE MARTIN
© 1999 Joe Martin.

CATS WITH HANDS
JOE MARTIN

PORTERFIELD

BY JOE MARTIN

"I'M GOING TO ALLOW YOU THIS DEDUCTION ... BUT ONLY FOR A FEW MOMENTS"

"300 PEOPLE IN THE ROOM. YOU'D THINK ONE OF 'EM WOULD'VE YELLED 'DUCK!'"

"IN BUSINESS AND IN GOLF THE IMPORTANT THING IS 'FOLLOW-THROUGH.' NOW TAKE THIS CLUB, FIND PORTERFIELD AND REMEMBER WHAT I TOLD YOU"

"HOW IS IT WHEN THEY DO IT, IT'S A GREAT IDEA AND A MAJOR INNOVATION... BUT WHEN WE DO IT... IT'S PATENT INFRINGEMENT ?! "

" THERE GO THE RUMORMONGERS "

" WHAT SOUNDS BETTER...'IT'S LOST, GONE FOREVER, KISS IT GOODBYE'... OR...'IT'S IN THE SYSTEM'?"

" AND HERE'S THE WIFE AND I AT YOSEMITE ... "

"YOU COULD SAVE US BOTH A LOT OF RED TAPE IF YOU'D MAKE A BREAK FOR THE DOOR"

"PORTERFIELD.. THIS BLANK PIECE OF PAPER ... I FOUND IT ON MY DESK ... IS IT YOUR RESIGNATION?"

"THE PRESSURE MUST BE GETTING TO FULLBEAN... HE'S CHANGED SHIELDS THREE TIMES"

"THERE'S A NEW RULE... WE HAVE TO ANSWER THE PHONE ON THE FIRST RING NO MATTER WHO WE THINK IT IS"

"AND FROM THIS DAY FORWARD WE WILL STEAL ONLY FROM THE RICH!"
JOE MARTIN
ROBIN HOOD EXPLAINING THE "KEY ACCOUNT" CONCEPT

JOE MARTIN
"IT'S SO EASY TO CRITICIZE OTHER PEOPLE... MAYBE THAT'S WHAT I'LL DO TODAY"

HE WAS AN IDIOT TO SAY SOMETHING THAT STUPID IN THE FIRST PLACE
BZZZZZZZZZ

JOE MARTIN
"PORTERFIELD.. THIS MUMBO-JUMBO IN ARTICLE 16... CHANGE IT BACK TO HOCUS-POCUS"

"WELL..SOMEONE'S GOT TO TELL HIM...AND THE SOONER THE BETTER!. IT'S GOING TO BE HARD ENOUGH THE WAY IT IS"

" PORTERFIELD.. WE CAN NO LONGER AFFORD TO PAY YOU... BUT YOU'RE WELCOME TO STAY ON AS A FRIEND "

"DO YOU WANT TO TELL HIM OR SHOULD I ?"

" EITHER THEY'RE NOT HERE OR THEY'RE HIDING... EITHER WAY IT'S A BAD SIGN "

" EVERY TIME HE TELLS IT THERE'S MORE 'BLAMS' "

" THEY SELL THEM AT THE OFFICE SUPPLY STORE... THEY'RE A LITTLE MORE IF YOU WANT A DIFFERENT NAME"

" WE'VE SOLD 2 MILLION GALLONS OF 'HARVEST GOLD'.. 4 MILLION GALLONS OF 'ROBIN'S EGG BLUE' AND 8 MILLION GALLONS OF 'CANARY YELLOW' BUT WE'VE YET TO SELL ONE CAN OF YOUR 'TOILET WHITE' "

"I'LL TELL YOU THE TRUTH.. I'D KIND OF HOPED 'VOODOO CURSE' WOULD'VE BEEN FURTHER DOWN THE LINE THAN 'PLAN B' "

"NOW REMEMBER, BOYS.. I GAVE THEM MY WORD ON THIS DEAL, SO AT LEAST WE DON'T HAVE TO WORRY ABOUT GETTING LOCKED INTO SOMETHING WE CAN'T LIVE WITH"

"NOW DON'T EVERYBODY TALK AT THE SAME TIME BUT... WHAT WOULD WE DO WITHOUT PORTERFIELD ?"

"TODAY I LOST THE ANDERSON ACCOUNT, THE BINKLEY ACCOUNT, THE COLDFIELD ACCOUNT, AND THE DEMPSTER ACCOUNT... TOMORROW I MEET WITH EABLEMAN"

" BOYS...WE'VE LOST OUR COMPETITIVE EDGE... THAT DESIRE AND WILL TO WIN!.. BUT ON THE PLUS SIDE, I DON'T THINK IT MATTERS "

"ON THE OTHER HAND IT'S KIND OF REFRESHING TO DEAL WITH A PROBLEM THAT HAS NOTHING TO DO WITH CASH FLOW "

" THEN IT'S AGREED.. WE'LL CALL UP TO MAKE THE OFFER BUT WE'LL HANG UP AFTER THE FIRST RING "

" ONE MAN'S TEA IS ANOTHER MAN'S POISON.. BUT THEN, THAT WAS BEFORE QUALITY CONTROL"

"FULLBEAN CALLED, SIR... HE'S IN A MEETING"

"TAKE SPECIAL CARE, PORTERFIELD, NOT TO CROSS YOUR EYES WHEN YOU SAY 'MONEY,' IT SHAKES THEIR CONFIDENCE"

" FIRST TIME? "

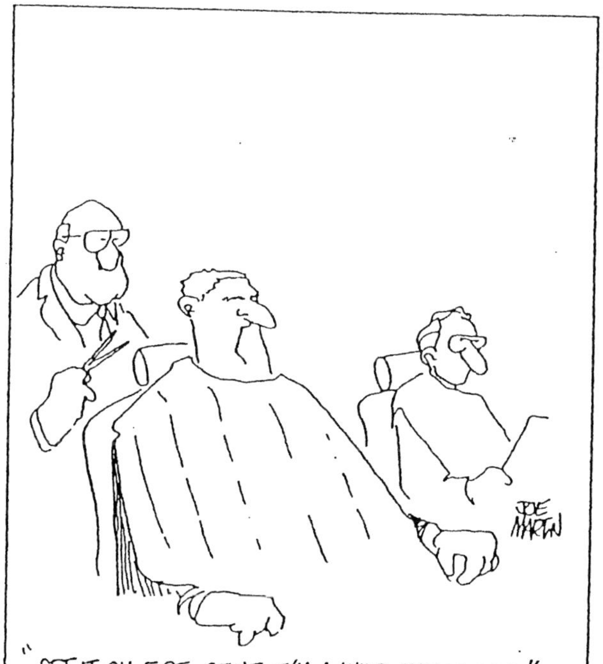

" SET IT ON FIRE, GENE, I'M A WILD MAN TODAY "

"YOU KNOW...IT'S A REAL SHAME, IN TIMES LIKE THIS THAT YOU CAN'T PUT A DOLLAR VALUE ON FRIENDSHIP"

"THE CAST WAS SO BAD WE FELL INTO THAT ALL TOO COMMON MISTAKE OF BUILDING THE SHOW AROUND ONE OF THE CAMERA MEN"

"PUT MORE MEN ON THE FEAZLEMAN CASE"

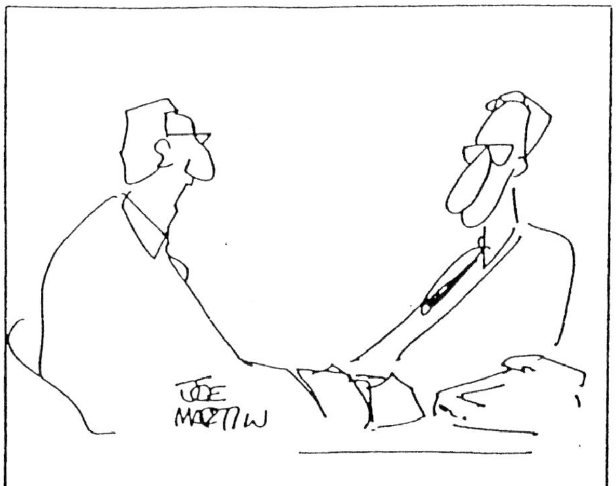

"SORRY, PORTERFIELD, BUT I'M AFRAID YOU'RE JUST A LITTLE TOO SLOW ON THE UPTAKE FOR FULLBEAN INDUSTRIES.. I THINK IT'S ABOUT TIME I TELL YOU. WHY YOU HAVEN'T BEEN GETTING YOUR CHECKS"

"OK.. HERE'S THE SAME DEAL UPSIDE DOWN... NOW WILL YOU TAKE IT?"

" NO, NO... LET ME GET IT "

WANNA BUY A COPY OF MY LATEST BOOK?.. "HOW I MADE A MILLION IN THE STOCK MARKET"...
IT'S GOT A SURPRISE ENDING

THE 12-MILLION-DOLLAR TYPOGRAPHICAL ERROR
ACE ICE CREAM
NEW!
IT'S RICH IT'S CREAMY
IT'S
PERCH COBBLER

MARTIN
"THEY WERE COUNTING ON ME AND I LET THEM DOWN... BIG DEAL"

PORTERFIELD
"THE BOSS WANTS YOU TO CLEAN OUT YOUR DESK AND CALL HIM WHEN YOU GET HOME... HE SAID IT WAS IMPORTANT"

"I THINK WE CAN ALL AGREE THAT INCREASING PORTERFIELD'S VACATIONS HAS BEEN, AT BEST, ONLY A TEMPORARY SOLUTION"

"'PRIVILEDGED INFORMATION,' MY FOOT! LOOK.. EVERYBODY KNOWS!!"

"I BROKE THE CARDINAL RULE OF BUSINESS: 'NEVER LET ANYONE KNOW YOU'RE AT THE WRONG MEETING'"

" ALL THOSE PEOPLE DOWN THERE... THOUSANDS AND THOUSANDS OF THEM AND NOT ONE OF 'EM KNOWS I BLEW THE BANCROFT ACCOUNT... WELL, MAYBE THE ONE DRIVING ON THE SIDEWALK "

" I CAN ALWAYS TELL... THIS IS ABOUT MONEY, ISN'T IT ? "

"FOR ONE BRIEF, SHINING MOMENT I WAS ONE OF THE WORLD'S RICHEST MEN ... BUT THAT'S ALL OVER NOW, THANKS TO AIRPORT SECURITY"

"I'M NOT READY TO JUMP OFF THE LEDGE YET.. BUT BY THE SAME TOKEN, I DON'T WANT TO BE THE LAST ONE OUT EITHER"

"YOU KNOW THAT AGGRAVATING THING OUR NEPHEW DOES WHERE HE KEEPS REPEATING EVERYTHING YOU SAY?... WELL, PORTERFIELD'S STARTING IT"

"WAIT.. BEFORE YOU MAKE THAT CHECK OUT, LET ME CALL HEADQUARTERS. WE MAY HAVE ALREADY COLLECTED ENOUGH AND YOU MIGHT NOT HAVE TO!"

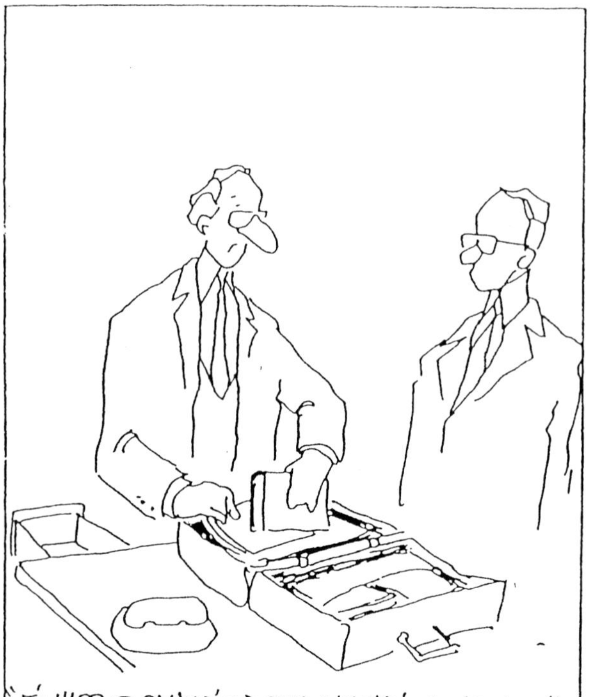

"IT'S HARD TO SAY 'NO' TO SOMEONE WHO'S FIRING YOU"

"PUT PORTERFIELD'S FILE UNDER 'J' FOR 'JERK' AND TAKE WHATEVER'S IN THERE AND PUT IT UNDER 'A-OK IN MY BOOK'"

"BY CHARGING FOR DIRECTORY ASSISTANCE WE WILL FORCE THEM INTO RANDOM DIALING... AND THAT, BOYS, IS WHERE THE BIG MONEY IS!"

INTERNAL REVENUE SERVICE
JOE MARTIN
"YOU COULD SAVE US BOTH A LOT OF RED TAPE IF YOU'D MAKE A BREAK FOR THE DOOR"

"PORTERFIELD.. THIS BLANK PIECE OF PAPER ... I FOUND IT ON MY DESK ... IS IT YOUR RESIGNATION?"

JOE MARTIN
"I COULD KICK MYSELF WHEN I THINK OF ALL THOSE NIGHTS I SPENT IN FRONT OF THE FIREPLACE"

J. MARTIN
"THERE'S A NEW RULE ... WE HAVE TO ANSWER THE PHONE ON THE FIRST RING NO MATTER WHO WE THINK IT IS"

"HE'S AN OK GUY IF YOU DON'T MIND SAYING 'EARTH TO FINSTHIEMER' EVERY 15 OR 20 SECONDS"

"IT'LL BE NICE WHEN I'M A FULL PARTNER AND I CAN HAVE MY <u>REAL</u> NAME ON THE DOOR"

"SOMETIMES I THINK IT WOULD BE BETTER IF THEY JUST TOOK IT AWAY"

"OH, C'MON..TOO MUCH OF ANYTHING WILL HURT YOU... BESIDES, WHO'S GOING TO DRINK A WHOLE BOTTLE?"

"PORTERFIELD, THEY'RE MAKING A COMPUTER THAT CAN DO EVERYTHING YOU DO...OR I SHOULD SAY MY KID IS"

"THEY GAVE ME A CHOICE ... EITHER RESIGN OR BE FIRED ... I TOLD THEM I'D DO WHATEVER I HAD TO TO KEEP MY JOB"

"THE DIFFICULT JOBS WE GIVE TO FORBES AND BARKER.. THE IMPOSSIBLE JOBS WE GIVE TO PORTERFIELD.. OR AT LEAST THAT'S THE WAY IT'S BEEN TURNING OUT"

"I'M IN FOR CREATIVE FINANCING... ACTUALLY IT'S ARMED CREATIVE FINANCING"

"MAINTENANCE MEN ARE 12 BUCKS AN HOUR, THESE SIGNS ARE PRACTICALLY FREE"

"SOME DAY THIS WILL ALL BE DONE BY COMPUTER"

"WE'RE LOSING A MILLION DOLLARS A DAY BECAUSE OF MIS DIRECTED ENERGIES . . . I WOULD KILL TO KNOW WHAT THAT WORKS OUT TO ON A PER-MINUTE BASIS"!

THE FOLLOWING ARE SICK, TASTELESS, DIRTY, FILTHY, PERVERTED AND OBNOXIOUS WITH NO REDEEMING SOCIAL VALUE WHATSOEVER
AND THESE, MISTER BOFFO, ARE THE HOGANS
WHAT DOES SHE THINK, I'M BLIND?!
I USED TO SEND THEM IN WITH MY REGULAR BATCH OF NEWSPAPER COMICS TO SEE IF THE EDITORS WERE REALLY READING MY STUFF...
ONE OF THEM MADE IT THROUGH WHICH IS WHY I DON'T DO IT ANYMORE
JOE MARTIN
ORF!

YOU CAN'T TEACH
AN OLD DOG
HOW TO FLY
JOE MARTIN

HOW SOON TILL WE CAN
CALL HIM "LEFTY"?

MISTER BOFFO
"STOP BOUNCING ON THE BEDS AND GET TO SLEEP!"
-NO. 3 ON LIST OF ORDERS LEAST HEARD IN PRISONS-
AND HIS WONDER-DOG "WEEDERMAN"
BY JOE MARTIN
DEAREST... I HAVE A CONFESSION TO MAKE...
I'VE BEEN SEEING GEORGE, OUR PLUMBER!
I NEVER THOUGHT A WOMAN COULD LOVE TWO MEN AT THE SAME TIME...
UNTIL HE INTRODUCED ME TO PHIL... HIS HELPER.
JOE MARTIN

"THERE IS ENOUGH ENERGY IN THE WARHEAD OF ONE NUCLEAR MISSILE TO HEAT ALL OF DOWNTOWN TOLEDO UNTIL IT MELTS"
AND HIS WONDER-DOG "WEEDERMAN"
BY JOE MARTIN
HUH!
CLONK
WUP!
HE MAKES IT LOOK SO EASY.
JOE MARTIN

YA KNOW, IN ALL THE YEARS I'VE BEEN DOING THIS I'VE YET TO MEET ONE THAT DIDN'T HAVE A BUG UP HIS ASS ABOUT SOMETHING

GUESS WHO FELL OFF THE BALCONEY AGAIN ?

MISTER BOFFO
"A MISSILE WITHOUT A NUCLEAR WARHEAD IS LIKE KISSING YOUR SISTER"
AND HIS WONDER-DOG "WEEDERMAN"
BY JOE MARTIN

ALCOHOLICS ANONYMOUS
FAMOUS DRUNKS SCHOOL

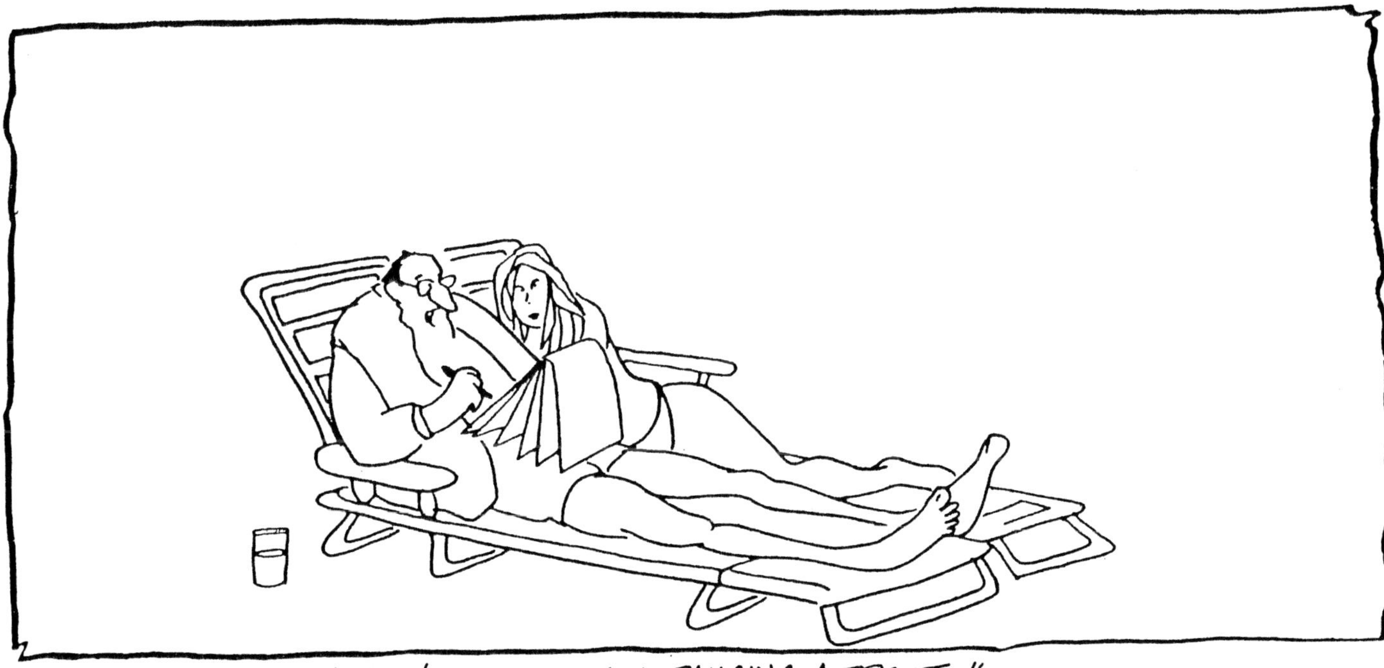

" HERE'S ONE OF YOU BANGING A TROUT "

AIN'T BUT ONE THING I LIKE BETTER'N A BIG FAT UGLY SMELLY WOMAN AND THAT'S ONE WITH A GUN

SODAS
SOMEONE TOLD THE PETERSON TWINS I WASN'T A GYNECOLOGIST!
JOE MARTIN

MUST MEAN "NUDIST COLONY AHEAD."
JOE MARTIN

NO, JOHNNY...
NOT HERE.. LOOK!!
NO
~~PARKING~~
PORKING
IT'S THAT WEASEL FENDERMAN!... I'LL GET HIM FOR THIS!!
JOE MARTIN

TROUBLE
CHARLES MANSON
REAL TROUBLE
HIS EVIL TWIN
JOE MARTIN

THE REALLY GREAT THING ABOUT MATTHEWS IS..NO MATTER WHAT HE SAYS IT WILL SCARE THE PANTS OFF OF 'EM, AND THAT'S HALF THE BATTLE!
JOE MARTIN

HEY... DORKFACE.. EAT ME !!
THE FIRST THING WE NEED, BENTON, IS A NEW PASSWORD !!

THE UNDERSEA WORLD OF COUSTEAU'S JOCK
SOAP

NOW, REMEMBER, MRS. JOHNSON.. JUST ONE ARTICLE AT A TIME.. AND PLEASE WAIT UNTIL I CHANGE THE RECORD
JOE MARTIN

TWO GEORGIA PEACHES AND A TENNESSEE SQUAT MELON

SWEATERS
SLA KS
LINGERIE

OK, JOHNSON.. I SHOT YOUR WIFE AND I SHOT YOUR KID... WHADDYA SAY TO THAT!
DID YOU KNOW I HAVE A DOG?
JOE MARTIN

WELL.. WOULD YOU MARRY ME IF I WASN'T AN ASSHOLE ?

ALL MY FRIENDS THINK I'M CRAZY
WHY DON'T YOU KILL THEM ?

BOFFO

JOE MARTIN

Printed in the United States
54166LVS00003BA/11-112